ELEMENTAL

RIVER PAW PRESS

Elemental
Copyright © River Paw Press, 2026

First Edition: 2026

ISBN: 979-8-9896607-6-6

Individual Poems
Copyrights © Individual Poets, 2026

Anthology Concept and Editing
Copyright © Kalpana Singh-Chitnis, 2026

Layout and Book Cover Design © Silent River
Cover Art © Silent River
Cover Image © Anja

River Paw Press

USA

www.riverpawpress.com

Elemental

2025
Earth Amulet Poetry Prize Anthology

Edited by

Kalpna Singh-Chitnis

Acknowledgements

We would like to extend our sincere thanks to our 2025 Earth Amulet Poetry Prize judges, Candice Louisa Daquin and Kalpna Singh-Chitnis, and to everyone who has supported the publication of the *Elemental* anthology.

The earth is you. You are the earth. When you realize there is no separation, you fall completely in love with this beautiful planet. ~ Thich Nhat Hanh

Table of Contents

Ashes

By Maryam Imogen Ghouth

Do not burn me to ashes
then pour me into a vase.
Let my body be food
for life-giving worms.

In place of my bones
a mighty tree might bloom,
and every time you eat
from its seeds and fruit

my atoms shall find
a loving home in you,
and in the rhythmic throb
of your beating heart,

you will carry the pulse
of a million lives,
for the fruit of me
is of a million more—

each will have eaten
the seeds and flesh
of a fruit once fed
by those before.

5:00 A.M.

By Maryam Imogen Ghouth

A different reality sets in
at 5:00 a.m.

You might hear the whoosh
of a solar flare,
the shudder of silence
in vacuum air,
the rat-a-tat of a distant star,

the low groan of black holes
spiralling toward a merger,
the violent bloom
as they collide into one another.

And if you tune into the now,
time may bend and bow—
you might catch the boom
of the first millennia,
a glimpse of an ancient mother,
the golden hour of the Tang empire,
or the moment that just went by.

The world hushes—
trees blanketed in mist,
birds curled in moonlit tryst.
This quiet joins you
by a seam to all that exists.

It calls you into being.

Every part of you attends,
unhindered, eager,
awaiting its turn
to applaud or lament.

Even foreign murmurs
you now decipher;

feelings appear
cleaner, sharper.
In this lucid hour,
you learn who you are:
a mortal, sober, alone—
held in the indifferent
swell of time.

No other human
to soften with addition,
to fool with separation.

It is not loneliness you feel,
but the vastness
of one.

To What Matters Most

By Maryam Imogen Ghouth

Isn't good just as bad
when taken to excess?

Imagine a bright world
with goodness overflowing:
a mass too big to contain.
Would we thrive,
or might we be dead—

as when too much water
kills the waiting roots,
yet, violent winds impel
trees to greater heights?

What if neither extreme
destroys its opposition—
in the way that the cosmos
ensures that neither
dark matter, which binds,
nor dark energy, which repels,
erases the other one?

Had dark energy been weak,
our universe may have re-collapsed
and we may have never lived
to contemplate its counter-weight.

Opposites
keep the balance.

Let dark energy repulse,
while matter clutches on
to what matters most.

It Grows

By Maryam Imogen Ghouth

Your love enters me
like light into leaf,
and I give it back as breath.

It thickens my veins
with green hope,
turns hunger into sugar
stored deep.

Years later and still, moisture rises unseen,
your gift turning my heat
into rain.

I lean toward you,
my body remade in colour,
until even my shade shelters the other.

At dusk you linger,
a glow held under.
In storm you steady,
my stem refusing to sunder.

Sometimes, I return your love
as blossom,
fruit in hand,
seed for tomorrow's ground.

And even when harvest is over,
I begin again—
season after season,
your love remade
like new rings forming.

The Gift Born of the Coincidence of Opposites

By Maryam Imogen Ghouth

Some truths I gathered through choice,
others through luck,
but stranger still are those that rose
when all within
was housed under one roof:
my order and disorder,
my glee and grief—
not favouring one over the other
but what their union could birth:

how tension, held between two sides,
might give rise to something else
in the way that the friction
between foot and ground
propels the body forth,
between egg and sperm
ushers a child to life,
between chaos and order
brings art to life—

as when the sweeping flood of sensation
and the borders of a daily regime—
time allotted, check-in, check-out,
sit your ass down and write—
meet to give the wild its form.

We swing, we shift,
we step foot
on either side of the line.
Even our sun
holds in her balance
the inward crush of gravity
and the outward force
of nuclear fusion.
She, too, is embroiled
in a war of her own,
and we are forged from a star;
this battle is inborn.

Fonio

By Vinita Agrawal

A grain so small
it holds the sky lightly.

It does not ask for rain,
only remembers it.

The soil here is tired,
but the fonio is not.

It grows where other grains turn away,
where the earth splits in the heat.

Survival is to bend without breaking,
to be ancient, but not fragile.

A child could spill a handful
and not know they held entire harvests,

generations of hunger
satiated between their fingers.

The women winnow it like whispers,
let the wind take what it needs.

When the fires come, the fonio waits.
When the floods pass, it remembers how to rise.

It does not boast about its resilience,
but simply grows.

This is how the universe began—
not with a star, but a seed.

Note: Fonio is an ancient, nutritious cereal grain (Digitaria exilis) native to West Africa.

Quantum Seed

By Vinita Agrawal

I am the maybe-plant, the not-yet-tree
a collapse of futures curled tight in my shell.
I am root and rot, bloom and wither,
You only see the shell.

The sparrow's beak, the shovel's turn,
the acid dark of a squirrel's cheek—
each touch unspools me into versions:
a stalk of wheat; a creek-side tangle of milkweed.

I do not choose. The wind decides.
The rain insists. Even your hand,
hovering midair,
is a Schrödinger's fist—

will you crush me, or cradle me?
The soil hums with ghosts of maybes:
a forest if I'm buried, a feast if I'm swallowed,
a crack in the concrete if I'm forgotten.

I am the experiment. The hypothesis.
The single electron spinning through
every possible orchard.
Observer, look close—

when you blink, I split again.

Sattal

By Vinita Agrawal

Seven whispers of water
stitched into earth's quiet hymn—
a mirror broken by the dip of wings.
A biome kept whole by chirping larynges.

Here, the trees hold their breath,
while a Himalayan bulbul turns the air to song,
while the Verditer Flycatcher brandishes
its turquoise in shallow pools.

A Kingfisher's blue flash—
just a ripple, then gone.
The Forktails dance
between shadow and stone.

Somewhere,
the Blanford's Rosefinch
unfolds its liquid notes,
and the pines lean closer to listen.

The lake does not hurry.
The sky does not falter.
Even time is just another bird
alighting softly on the shores of Sattal.

Note: Sattal is a popular birding site at the foothills of the Himalayas.

Late Summer Stanza

By Scott W. Westcott

Opening night, for the cicadas
the orchestra assembled
in towers of leafy oaks
their violins in sing-song harmony
see-sawing back and forth
relentlessly

Remarkable, if you think about it,
these creatures, ancient as they are,
know nothing of this world.
Nothing of the problems in this house,
and the other houses, here in Pheasant Hill Farms
The resentments, betrayals, all simmering
Decades-old report cards buried under mattresses
Dishes and dishes upon dishes
piling in the sink

Much less the bigger stuff – artificial intelligence, chatbots
war, famine, Taylor Swift, Trump
climate change, that one day could
silence this symphony,

Or not
Perhaps cicadas are the sole survivors
at very least those that enjoy a 17-year sleep
Awakened, emerging
oblivious to colossal catastrophe
Preparing to perform for a barren planet
An apocalyptic wasteland
with days of the deepest quiet

The cicadas, know nothing of this --
or anything else

Listening, I wonder,
when the night's final movement
concludes and cicadas bow
to dawn's soloists:

The cardinal's song, the sparrow's cheep
coos of mournful doves
and, lest we forget, the screeching caws of crows
hellbent on drowning it all out
Jealous bastards

Now I picture a gaunt grandmother
skeletal, buried under winter blankets,
yet still shivering
Before lights out
she'd asked the window be cracked, just a smidgen
to hear them play this night
Lying there
Listening and remembering, listening and remembering
remembering, remembering, remembering
until the remembering-pain
hurts more than bone-deep cancer ache

Then she recalls earlier, the cicada husk
on the windowsill
When that nice curly-haired aide guided her by elbow
to see "the beautiful blue summer sky!"
and of course, *to get your daily exercise*

Oh, that husk!
A perfect mold of its recent inhabitant,
lucky enough to shed its skin
How might she go about pulling off such a trick?
Soon, she thinks, soon
please, soon

Outside, in the darkness, unseen by this woman,
or anyone
A single browning leaf flutters free, high from the oak
Lower, an owl sharpens its gaze
clenching taloned feet
clutched to a branch
The mice below appear more industrious this night,
scurrying this way and that
Cicada symphony drowns owl's wing-whoosh
It's coming, the woman thinks, the cold,
the cold is coming

What the Universe Tells Us

By Scott W. Westcott

Full moon glows
bright as a day unfolding
in black-and-white
Bright enough to lift
an armada of impatient geese
from wheatfield stubble
Rush of wings
whooshing just over treetops
Urgent honks trumpet
of something
not quite right

Tempted to interpret this as an omen,
a cryptic warning from above
to soothe my ominous mind
and absolve myself of any responsibility
for the conduct of my species
But to pin this on these birds
places unfair blame on the universe
To the raven, your windowsill
is nothing more
than a convenient perch

All this assigning meaning
to the meaningless
only distracts from the cold cruel truth
of our own making
And just as I make a vow
to commit to this rationality,
and congratulate myself on
such keen insight
a brilliant cardinal has the nerve
to settle on a branch
but a few feet from my Adirondack chair
quizzically cocking his head
as he bounds branch to branch
closer and closer

What could it be
he so desperately wants to tell me?
Speak now, beautiful bird
I'm listening
I can handle the truth

Night Fishing

By Scott W. Westcott

Come early September
Steelhead sneak close to shore
But only in night's darkest hour
Drawn by Autumn's first flutters of homecoming

Imagine a crooked bony finger, beckoning them back, back,
back to the very stream's mouth that spits them forth
as fingerlings slimmer than minnows they devour
to grow sleek, silvered strong
waving, waving through cool bottom waters.

Fleeting are these nocturnal patrols
cruising clear of shaggy coastline
The first blush of late-summer dawn
hastens a swift retreat
Too soon, too soon

Knowing this, I set an ungodly alarm
Clumsy-stumble toward heart-swish of lapping waves
then, inching over slick-mossed rocks until water's waist high
Even a headlamp's glimmer can spook them back
So I'm left to cast into black abyss
listening for soft splash of a silvery spoon
Fanged and barbed deceiver
Ever so careful are these cast and retrieves
knowing the slightest tangle
ends this venture cold

Then the sudden jolt, hooked
Reel howling as the fish
freight trains toward the deep
Let it run, patience, tight line, tip high
Suddenly an uncertain easing foretells
the furied leap, shimmy-shake, splashdown
The fiery stuff of Field & Stream covers
left only to my mind's eye

Hook holds, hearts race as
our dark dance resumes, me and this fish
connected by thread-thin monofilament
Conflicting desire, clashing instincts
playing out an ancient heartbreak
How this ends will reveal Autumn's omen
Neither fish, nor I, shall speak of it

Hawk's Shadow

By Scott W. Westcott

A hawk's shadow
traces swiftly across the lawn
wings like flinty knives
slicing stillness
foreshadowing certain death
from a bloodless assault
executed
amid the flapping flush
of the spared
this time

Only a few stray feathers
remain
still perfection
clinging to grass and
to the shock, yet again, of
the knowing accomplice
who moments before
hummed happily while
filling feeders
clucking a sing-song call
beckoning eager
songbird
and hungry hawk
alike

Inchworm

By Scott W. Westcott

The easy, the logical, today
would be to write of darkness
interrogating the thickening gloom
that pervades
But that would betray the inchworm
that just achieved a heroic
unseen climb up my wrought-iron chair
to now seize-relax-seize-relax
over and over
across my forearm, enroute to
destination unknown, yet
purposefully moving every inch
of an inch-long body
Such commitment
such splendor
deserves accounting for
Today

Honorable Mentions

Sorcerer's Dance

By Alexander Scott Baker

Above the cliffs, the drifting clouds drift slow,
They bend and break in silver, gray, and gold;
The waves below fold in and fold out, so
They speak in hush of stories never told.
O sea, O pulse, O wind that shapes the strand,
O voice that lifts the water, lifts the land,
Thy rhythm rocks the heart, both young and old.
He moves where foam and dying sunlight blend,
A braided shape of salt, of sky, of air;
His antlers flash like lightning without end,
A crown of shadow, half of flame, half prayer.
No cave confines, no walls can keep him near;
The ocean hums the truths we only hear,
And time dissolves in brine, dissolves in care.
The wind and wave weave round him, round and round,
Their slanting hymns a thread both soft and strong;
The spray, a veil, falls silver, falls with sound,
A bridge of flesh and cloud, of wave and song.
He sways, he bends, yet never breaks the line,
A pulse of life, half mortal, half divine,
A secret sung, yet sung for all along.
We watch, yet centuries like currents roll,
The shimmer caught, then lost, then caught again;
The sky, the surf, the tides that pierce the soul,
All thread him through with green and foam and rain.
The wild, the calm, the voice we cannot see,
Conspire to mark the shape we're meant to be,
And in that dance our spirits rise, remain.

Answer to the Timaeus

By Alexander Scott Baker

You spoke of elements four in hand,
That shaped the heavens at command,
Of spheres that turn by craftsman's art,
And laws that bind the cosmic heart.
But I have seen the forests flame,
And rivers dance with none to name;
The lion roars, the sparrow sings,
No god has taught them such bright things.
The stars you fix in crystal skies
I know as fires in children's eyes;
They flare, they falter, fade away –
Not one is bound to endless day.
You praise the order, neat, divine,
Yet chaos is the greater sign;
For thunder breaks, and blossoms grow,
And none may tell the way they flow.
The soul you bind to astral flame
Leaps free, untamed, without a name;
It burns in joy, it breaks in pain,
It dies, it rises, lives again.
The world is not a statue still,
But living pulse, unfettered will;
The field, the storm, the bird in flight –
These mock your cold, mechanic night.
Your cosmos shines with measured grace,
But I behold a wilder face:
Where love and terror weave their thread,
And life outdances all the dead.

We Are No Longer Mythopoets

By Jharna Choudhury

The branches do not understand the birds anymore.

Our house sparrows stitch nests with fibre cables;
woodpeckers peck brown plastic shreds
as gods vacated their hollow.

When we were little girls,
our mothers left their milk for the trees to drink,
 bent and circled threads,
touched bark, felt a heartbeat,
cried in their shade a lullaby older than language.

Now, when I walk past the old bazaar temple
the yogis cough under the banyan trees,
the figs are overripe with flies in a black prayer;
the river stands song-less, frozen with ash,
as if something has been withdrawn—

perhaps, the village hymn, once sung together,
fragrance of real jasmine without the choke of smoke,
pigeons finding homes in the niches of old statues.
Now, stones are only stones.

From the Airport

By Jharna Choudhury

The glass felt cold; it shook my head.
I looked out at the asphalt stretch, like a knife
cutting my terracotta memories.

The jackfruit blossoms are replaced by hoardings
and signs that said *slow down*;
apartment pillars are upright like bones atop wetlands
once green with gossipy birds.

The sun rose, the herons didn't turn up,
the egrets and the straited grassbirds, their reedland
gone;

did the sky erase the maps of the bar-headed geese?

I saw a line of peepal stump like C-section scar of a mother
who delivered a stillborn.
Malls, warehouses, overbridge debris,
manicured palm trees in coloured pots,
and cattle looking for shade.

I carry a ball of earth in my throat,
a grief,
and I am the architect.

California Fire

By Diane Funston

Birds return to blackened trees
now cracked open with nourishment
Snow flowers bloom bright red
rise from ash in flamboyant assertion
foxes and bears roam the charred landscape
a settling-in follows
population again grows

Humans scatter far
Homes burned
prices gouged
as they migrate to cities
away from forests where
they inserted themselves

Avarice rebuilds what fire claims
again and again
No learning curve
Buy land
Build houses
Create isolated businesses
and wait...

for the match to strike again

Earth Forgives

By Diane Funston

Earth forgives
Forests rise after fires
Rivers push new tributaries
sluice into dry basins
Drought forces Darwinism
Flora and fauna adapt
or perish
Deep caves
spawn sightless fish
Mammals drink mere drops of moisture
Earth forgives
Tallies failure in fossils
written in stone
spreads winged success
in rainbow parrots
over grayer skies

Melt

By Gloria Heffernan

Some memories have already
begun the inevitable melt
like glaciers calving into the sea.
What was the name of the iceberg
the size of Delaware that we photographed
from the cruise ship window?
How many countries signed
the Antarctic Treaty and when does it expire?
Already, I have forgotten
the markings that distinguish
the gentoo penguin from the Adelie,
the longitude and latitude
of frozen ports of call,
how many days Shackleton's men
were marooned on Elephant Island.

I remember wonder.
I remember awe.
I remember the long slow sigh
of a humpback whale surfacing for air,
the clatter of penguins gabbling
in throngs on the beach
the roar of two cantankerous
fur seals crashing their chests together
like cymbals.

But I remember too, the days
when the temperature was warmer
than my hometown half a world away.
I remember the thunder of ice walls
crashing into the blue waters of Paradise Bay.
I remember days when I peeled off
the multiple layers of wool and fleece
I thought I would need in the coldest place on Earth.
I remember the ship's naturalist
explaining that one point on the thermometer
would decimate the krill population and starve

the whales that depend on them for food.
And I remember how the snow
in my backyard never simply melts.
It recedes — gradually at first
until suddenly, without fanfare,
it's gone.

Meditation on the Northern Lights

By Gloria Heffernan

I saw the Northern Lights tonight,
pointing the way to Ojibwa country
where giveaways free the soul
of its earthly burdens,
and *miigwech* is the word
for thank you.

Halfway between Milwaukee
and Lac du Flambeau,
we pulled over to the shoulder of the road
to watch the lights rise up across the sky

waving in shimmering sheets
of iridescent green
like the wings of a million lunar moths
flying headlong into the stars.

I saw the Northern Lights tonight,
and when a mere thank you
simply wouldn't do.
I borrowed that word,
Miigwech,
as mysterious, as luminous
as those lights.

My pulse beats in time
with that cosmic ballet,
a gift too vast to be contained,
impossible to bear alone,
So I pass the memory on to you,
a giveaway of sorts,
unburdening my soul
from the weight
of an unshared story.

The Abandoned Places Nature Reclaims

By Larry Kilman

There was a road here once, all signs erased
Except for the verdant canopy
And parallel lines of even-spaced trees, in timeless obeisance.

In the dim light, the track itself is faint, as if made by deer,
No trace of wagon wheels or the clatter of hoofbeats.
A ghostly avenue raising more questions than answers, a dark cathedral.

Phototropism is at work here, but so are human hands,
Creating beauty by imposing order on the natural world.
Plantings born of a desire for pattern and control.

It is a birthright, provided by divine providence,
A responsibility to make sense of profundity,
A way of saying I am master of all I see.

Even the trees behave.

These avenues appeal to something deep within us, measured and refined.
It is why live oaks dripping Spanish moss line the entrance to the golf course
And processions of beech and poplars lead to manor houses.

So too the colonnades of jacarandas in winter resonate,
Holding promise of violet blooms and perfume
And better times when the rain comes.

And why plane trees mark the route through the French countryside,
Keeping time as cars click by. It is our nature, this geomancery,
Reordering the world so we are not overwhelmed.

It is a kind of immortality. The road through the woods is gone,
The mansions are rubble, the people are in the ground.
But the trees endure, still standing, in search of the sun.

Up The Mountain

By Larry Kilman

The green quiet of the country, somber in the rain,
so benign and beautiful, yet somehow sinister,
beauty and mystery both, ferns and wildflowers,
birdsong and the chatter of crickets and cicadas.

The air is soft in summer, the forest serene,
criss-crossed by hard-packed roads, trees bending in supplication,
creating a tunnel in deep shadow that narrows in the distance.

A spruce bog over the next rise, dappled yet clear enough
to see the mountains reflected and impressionistic,
the world stood on its head. Two plastic chairs
are poised at the edge in defiance of mosquitos.

Beyond this profuse chaos, regimented beauty;
precise stone and clapboard, forthright homes and churches,
black-and-white photos come to life,
extending through time, place and the seasons.

Yet obscurity everywhere, buried in mist and ambiguous weather.
Beauty is often accompanied by its opposite.
Skulls carved in headstones, names and dates
shrouded in darkness, small graves of children,
some sunken below the grade. Gargoyles on chimney pots,
bad omens in need of purging?

Hawks circling, crows gathered in twilight by the railroad tracks,
wings held close to the vest. They seem to be waiting,
just waiting, turning to regard passersby, as if to say,
Wilderness can be a wicked master.

A drunken-throated warble from the neighbor,
loud enough to carry the river,
Is it ecstasy or pain?

In winter, sunlight streams through branches
enfolded in crystal after the storm,
casting diamonds in the snow.

History Lesson from the Land

By Margie B. Klein

This land is ancient, antediluvian in origin,
the tale preserved in rock and stone.
In a museum-like climate, the traces remain.
There was life here before the colonizers came.
Pictographs and petroglyphs, messages
from the past - sprayed on, chiseled in,
rock art and artifacts teach a hands-on
history lesson to those who wish to learn.
Ichthyosaur, the lizard-fish
swam over these parched lands,
relics from the past left behind
from a shining sea which once
covered the desert bare,
now scattered dry lake beds left
where the ground rose and water fell.
Fossil hunters delight to find
seashell impressions and trilobites,
prehistoric riparian plants imprinted
in sandstone, limestone and shale.

A once-running wash and spring beds sport
archeological finds that researchers dream of -
skeletons of mammoths, and saber-toothed cats
lie in shallow graves in the riverbed cuts.
From eons earlier dinosaur prints –
though they won't tell you where they are.
Don't want anyone hacking them out
of the rock just to put in their yards.
It's the same with rock art carefully
carved by indigenous hands over time -
blasted out quickly to decorate
a mansion of the nouveau riche.
Eons of history wiped out, who cares?

Paint another one - no one knows,
authentic or not, sells for a good price
at less than genuine tourist traps.
More recent are the tread tracks from
Patton's tanks on a practice run, reminders
of how long it takes the desert crust to heal.
This age-old land is persistent but delicate,
enduring but fragile, to be traveled with respect.

Scents and Sensibility

By Margie B. Klein

The desert has sense
we humans can't fathom…
wisdom and connections from
an ancient way of life.
Eking out a living
in an abrasive setting,
the sense of the desert
is caught in its scents.

When they say it smells like rain,
it's the scent of earth itself -
petrichor from living microbes,
chemicals catalyzed when
wet offerings are made.
Creosote smells oily and sharp.
Wild snapdragon so sweet
you can almost taste it.
Desert willow blooms lightly floral,
cheesebush is tart and spicy.
On a summer's eve, sagebrush
smells minty, refreshing your nostrils
from the acrid stench of rotting carbon,
stagnant rock and mummified corpses -
the minerals in the desert varnish
release an odor when they're heated up -
that burning smell of singed fiber
and the smell of absolutely nothing,

Four more senses than smell -
opened wide in undisturbed desert,
reward you with epiphanies.
Alert ears hear cactus wren and quail.
Desert wind sounds like a whispering voice.

Vistas so wide, horizons blur mountain to valley.
The discovery of tiny plants you get on your belly to see.
Low to the ground – you can almost feel
the pulse of the earth's core below.
With heightened awareness, you can
detect grains of sand being flicked
away as a reptile moves.

Nature sense is when we receive
the signals provided by the outdoors
through all our senses and understand
the knowledge that's contained within
by the way all of them together make us feel.
The desert offers a delicate buffet
for sampling, with flavors both
subtle and intense, always warm.
Desert intuition contained
in its essences – once you experience
it, you won't want to forget.
Enter the ambedo cloud and come alive.

Abscission

By Molly O'Dell

Your golden beech leaves gleam
in winter's wood. Restrained
and faded, serrated shapes offer

a final flitter above eye level,
long after witch hazel blooms
dwindle and drop. Throughout

winter your clasp on stems resists
the winds. Pale fronds flap flutter
and fold. Clinched and shriveled

marcescence perseveres until, at last
you let go of last year, claims
on your axis, what you've always done.

When days lengthen, but before
red-winged blackbirds nest,
resins beckon you to ripen,

sever that hold. Decay gives
way to abscission and new
gifts of tender green flesh.

Ode to Roadkill Collector

By Molly O'Dell

With tussled dark hair and long slender
legs you step out of the work truck
in the middle of a primary two lane.
Beneath a green reflector vest, your

gloved hand peels a raccoon from asphalt.
Guts dangle as you sling the carcass
into the back of the truck atop three or
four blood covered deer. I think I glimpse

a bear head between some broken legs.
I have looked for you many long years
on endless pavements of by-ways
and highways. Today's my first sighting.

Your office is the side of the road. Alone
you work with truck and shovel. Skills
required are two: a valid driver's permit
and the ability to withstand stench from

active decay and maggots. Job openings
abound, decent pay by hour or animal. Earn
seventy-five grand a year. You stoop to keep
roadways clean, lay our wild friends to rest.

Gruinard Island

By Caroline Anne Pollard

The sky has stolen the
sea — thief of its hue.
The sea is bacterium
blue. The sky turns
bitter as sloes.
A gaunt tree stands
with Wyllie's spire-its
poverty of leaves
grieves.

Coarse gorse and the
bilberry stain of
heather. Weather:
force six gales. Black-
headed gulls sing as
sirens, their wings
flutter like lost sails.

Contagious swarms
of midges' cloud like
the black pollen of
spores. The island
weeps a brown burn.
This seizure of
seawater cannot heal
this raw wound.

The molten *aurum* of
a sunset coats the
recurring tide. Flecks
of gold filigree hide
the salt crests of
waves.

This landscape
becomes pure
alchemy — like the

alchemy of disease,
that transmutes spirit
to matter, the soul to
cells.

An empty boat is
tethered to the island
by its mooring rope,
tug-tugging on its
umbilical cord to hell.

Like engineered
destinies – the spell of
these architects of
fate, who dare wear
mock angel feet in the
playgrounds
where gods meet.

Seascape

By Caroline Anne Pollard

A periwinkle sky floats
on a raucous sea,
and splits
like oil on water.
The horizon bisected
by its bogus infinity.

Shore and sky prise open
like the
shell of a razor clam.

An opalescent moon hangs heavy
in a tarnished,
mother-of-pearl sky,
sea thrift pink pales into rose gold,
split
by the indecision of its iridescence.

Like the detritus of driftwood, it is
polished to art.
The old bones of shells lie empty as
graveyards.

A curlew plucks at the salt-encrusted
sand flats, as its Giacometti shadow
lengthens beyond,
frail,
elegance,

until it is no more than the
penumbra
of a
starved shadow.

The darkness rushes in and floods
the sand with a convulsion
of water.

The tide's déjà vu that
never truly repeats—
fluxing,
fixed by its impermanence.

Clouds

By Stephen Sanders

I know what you are—
precious water condensing in midair
on billions of particles of dust or
trillions of specks of pollen.
Another miracle we all accept as reality.
But I can understand you better
if I write your name in my memories.
The wounded summer storm you carried
in your arms from my east to my west.
Your grandeur, reflected in the water
at my boots, as the sea washes
the blood from the sand. The shape
and color of my mother's face
as she lay dying and I could no longer
bear to watch her doing it. Staring
into the red and gold as your mansion
burns gloriously to the ground, to blackness.
Finding you again at Key West
or Bolivar or the Grand Canyon,
reaffirming the power and depth of my love,
knowing it will be with me forever,
just like this sky, just like this moment,
just like my memories of you.

The Light of a Million Lamps

By Stephen Sanders

Midnight: greasy, black smoke erupts
heavenward from a blazing Hades amidships,
the brick oven inferno powering our industry.
I sweat, suspended over the bloody hulk
of a once-mighty whale. The huge carcass
rolls over and over beneath
the precarious plank on which I toil.
The lifeless leviathan shrinks
as I use my cutting spade to strip
thick blankets of rubbery fat
from the bloody corpse. The blubber,
sliced into "books," slithers quivering
into the trypots to be melted down.
If I take a false step? Into the bloody sea
with the sharks, never to return.
If I am careless with my razor-sharp spade?
I could lose a foot or slice muscle to the bone.
Spill the scalding, molten blubber
on hands, face, or legs?
I might never sail again, never work again.
It is all so horrible, so dark, so dangerous.
But shy, young sweethearts will share
glancing smiles under the soft glow
of lamplight on the streets of
Boston, San Francisco, and New York.

Fiery Eyes

By Ron Shapiro

Children smile
As constellations tumble
To Earth and dissolve
Into dust.

Even in darkness
When the moon appears to
Vanish, birds spread wings
To thread their flight over
Waterfalls, treetops in forests
Before landing by the muddy
River where the water flows
To the sea.

In the quiet of night,
Underground fungi
And mycelium curve around
Roots, rocks and decaying
Logs as soft as an angel's
Wings.

Can you hear voices
Of the wind helping you
To remember the secret
Of the quiet fire flickering
In your heart?

You are no island
Made of stone, pale and grey
Like death. Nothing here to
Imitate, to smother what can
Be imagined, what can be
Heard in this gallery of
Painted voices?

No doors to hide behind,
No windows to shut,

No tongue to hold,
No cage to blacken your
Motionless bones.

When the book falls from
The shelf and you discover
This gift of words leaping
Off the page and into your
Blazing hands, the secret
Which has always been
Known will reveal your
Wildness in a glimpse
From your fiery eyes.

Mountains and Sand

By Ron Shapiro

Lament the mountains
Where shepherds roam
For days without a map
Listening to the earth's
Message not to forget
What was never taught
In school: be not afraid
To question why what is
Now full will change to
Emptiness. As water
Evaporates into
Thundering clouds,
Learn to see the border
Of circles that spiral
And swirl into space.
Look for the sign near
The old farmhouse where
Grandfather used to wave
At the rain streaking across
The field. His thumb pointing
To where his eyes see. What
Happened to the wilderness?
He asks then yawns. A fire
Burns in his belly when he
Thinks about the sadness
Of mountains looking down
On the ravaged landscape.
If trees could fly, he muses,
Would they do a final dance
Then take flight into the cerulean sky
Leaving behind a single seed, the size
Of a single grain of sand?

Night Rain

By Jonathan Ukah

The day was going well with the sun;
there was no sign of dispute in the sky
before the clouds wore grave clothes
as though they lost their loved ones last night.
A bevy of swans drove through the trees
and the streets were empty of shadows.
The rain arrived with light affliction,
high decibels of thunder, flashes of lightning,
multicoloured streaks rode across the sky.

The rain poured down in fat pellets,
like long bamboo dividing the air,
while I remembered the drones of yesterday
that shredded our house like a bombed city.
My mother sighed a thousand times in a second.
My father urged us to hide in the plantation.
But the wind did not provide us with a cover.
My mother grabbed a bucket, my sister a broom.
I rushed out to stare at the sky like a rainmaker.

When the flood ran over our house,
we were like those who dropped from the sky,
with neither a lineage nor loved ones;
we were chickens struck by lightning,
paralysed like the chilled eggs of swans,
awaiting the breaking hour to arise
and save us from the pendulum.
But my father grabbed a long shovel;
my mother scooped balls of water.

The Garden of Bones

By Jonathan Ukah

The rays of the sun found a way into our garden
though the wind's maze was floating around.
My mother was there to harvest wilted grass,
leaves fallen from the weariness of time,
when there was no rain and no air,
where flowers withered for lack of light
after the sun had withdrawn its grace
and darkness covered the greying fields.
My mother bowed to the ground with pain,
for the end of the war that cost our heads,
the plants and flowers that malnourished.

Lying on the grass in the middle of our garden
as though imploring the grace of Heaven
to send down a chariot to lift it high,
was a piece of a black bone of a man's leg
displayed to the trees without a camouflage.
My mother shrieked at the unusual sight,
turning to stare at it with wrinkled brows.
A thousand ways to leave a bone behind
hanging between the clouds and the grey fields,
wondering what crimes, what evil against blood
did the bone commit for a lack of charity?

Perhaps a former soldier of the rising sun,
slain like a lamb at an unworthy sacrifice;
or it's the part body of a deadly hero
who had slaughtered a thousand other heroes
and chewed their bones like green herbs?
Or the bone of a one-eyed and one-armed
shot in the chest while unable to dive into a corner.
A thousand days must have eclipsed the light,
after the holocaust, bones drained their blood,
and now lie in my mother's garden breathless
as the remembered relic of a forgotten war,

What deep memories did the bone inhabit,

what heavy dreams has it forever foregone?
Fighting for victory for those blessed with flesh,
while the chasms of life widened at its intervals
when time eclipsed the desire of the righteous,
did rain and thunder shriek its wonder to rise?
What love did it abandon, what heartbreak,
when full blossom rested on its hot blood?
Perhaps it stepped on the inimitable Ogbunigwe
saved millions of lives and their gaudy destinies
and now lies there like a stalk of dead rose?

The Word for *Word* in Ocean

By William Weissinger

Across thirty-five miles of fetch, long swells heft in
from the south-southeast to a seaside cove.
The cove bounces back perfect arcs of waves

to the southwest, waves so small they'd barely bother
a thigh-deep wader. Wavelets arcing east southeast
criss-cross the waves, and if one focuses only on

the wavelets then for a moment only they arc across
the cove – the orchestra pausing for the piccolo.
Now I look not at the swells or waves or wavelets

but at where they cross and intersect to form water-
sculpted symbols that evoke Chinese characters,
script of ever-changing messages, writing and rewriting

and rewriting them out. The ocean speaks Seagull.
The ocean speaks Goose and Loon, Seal and Salmon,
Orca and Humpback, Squid and Clam, Mussel and Oyster,

but not yet me. What does it say with every swell?
Raise the portcullis. Open the gate.
I am ready to know its Word.

Even Though You Don't Believe in God

By William Weissinger

Like an odd brilliant thought you have as you
drive your little girl to Sunday School and she
asks a question and you answer but then
your thought is gone, simply no longer there,
a whale whooshes
and you look.
The long back
of a humpback
arcs into the sea,
disappears, is gone,
so you watch the sea.
You watch.

You watch.
You watch.
You watch,
but all you see
through the smooth water-
reflected whitish haze
of the sky
are a lone seal,
and one log –
motionless on the water,
as though time
has stopped.

The seal floats above
the undulating swells
as though holy.
You know it
really is resting
on a rock there
that's barely submerged.
The seal knows
it is safe and secure.
And you are too, you
and your curious child,

as safe and secure
as the seal, until
that log moves, until
time starts flowing again,
so you look and that log
is gone, gone without a trace,
as gone as your thought.

Notable Poems

Black Earth

By Diane Bier

Two and a half million people work the fields
feeding 340 million people in the US.

   Sweat soaked bandana faces feed families.
   Dropping named popsicle sticks in buckets.

Dropping to their knees from sunup to sundown.
Blistered, callused hands pulling red peppers—

   Scorched skin pulling green lettuce, cutting purple grapes.
   Migrant workers chased through rows of black earth.

Rotting in black earth are lush, leafy crops.
Famished children stare at food filled black earth.

   Black earth feeds people. Who feeds who? Migrants
   Feed your mouths with sweet, luscious berries.

Not all mouths filled with sweet, luscious berries.
Two and a half million people work the fields.

Two Old Oaks

By *Charles C. Gaines*

My little woodland is grieving
this spring as am I.
Two old oaks have failed
to survive the winter.
How many brutal winters
and heavy gales
did they withstand in their lives
How many hot dry summers?
How many thunderstorms,
How many long, dry droughts?
They stand tall, majestic as ever,
but not one speck of green
is on them;
nakedly forlorn
while the dance of new life whirls round.
The crows favor them as a roosting stop;
clear sightlines over
the verdant wilderness below.
Woodpeckers feast on their trunks.
Still useful, even in death.
Beneath, small saplings
rise above the undergrowth,
the promise of a successor or two,
should they survive.
New life arising from acorns
which found purchase and nurture
in the woody compost
layered in the dappled shade below.
I'll not live long enough
to know if any of them succeed
as progeny of the giant pair;
mighty buttresses, intrepid bulwarks,
protectors of the glade.
I stand still for a very long time,
considering how similar
their lives and mine have been.

Fertilize

By Rebecca Herz

In the beginning there was nothing.
Your absence echoed,
our hopes, fragmented.

Your absence hurt far more than the shots of hormone
she pressed, over and over, bruising herself.

In the clinic, you were a case study, a procedure,
a bundle of cells. Our fifth try,

you were never statistic, could not be counted
by two weeks' wait, or by pregnancy test.

When we found out you were
viable, it was outerbody.
You were a vision of cells on screen,

the first version of you we allowed ourselves to love.

Experience says, proceed with caution;
we know you're not here for us.

Experts seek your likelihood in data.
Science wants to measure your bone, find your heartbeat.

We have no idea what any of their lingo means.

Research gave us the chance to build your registry, open up
your pack 'n play, pin up pictures of your latest scan. To love

what was never ours, not really. I hypothesize;
The lab merged seeds only the sublime can fertilize.

The Forest

By Doc Janning

The forest
Rooted in the timeless wisdom of Earth
dreams
of time and peace
speaks
the silent philosophy of life
in the ancient tongues of the stars

It shares its essence
in a breezy psithurism
proclaiming an ancient future
in a present past

It exists
in the profound everchanging
Tao Zen and understanding
of the world within the world

And it shares its knowledge
and the age-old memories of the Earth
with those who are willing to listen

Are you of those who are willing

The forest

waits.

Canceled Ball

By Maryna Krazhova

Apparently, warmer winters are colder-hearted.
It's not the vitamin D deficiency,
not the deflated dusk,
or seasonal affective disorder,
but the unbearable bereavement of snow.

Sadness comes from scantiness:
from naked streets,
from roots exposed and stagnant,
      from the deep horizon,
         from unadorned mountains,
        bare stumps,
       nude roofs,
     clean roads.

The eye is thirsty for a cue of glitter.
Awe numbs without a splash of shapes.
The hunger for resplendent frost
is subtle, yet relentlessly persistent.
The dark grows darker,
Wistful turns to wretched.

At 6 p.m., the flashlight beams into nowhere.
The streetlight naps above the cancelled ball
of sparkles, snowflakes, icicles, and shadows.
The rainstorms yell outside
    for no-show snow.

I Call It Sycamore

By Elizabeth Iannaci

The tallest poem outside shivers
in the constant breeze, peeks
into my second-story window. I call
it Sycamore, yet I know it's really
a bee-tree. One day, it started
to sizzle like a thousand Lilliputian
kazoos, oscillating, making
the frightened wind hesitate, hide
in the canyon. Haz-Mat suited
workers came, gently trapped
the sound with gloves & hooks
& netting, turned it into a sea
of buzzes, ebbing. Now the wind
makes a home on branches, sounds
lonely, tries to frizzle, wheezing
as it blows the gypsy iris's pollen,
pretends it can make its own honey.

Lenses

By Mariana Mcdonald

If you can
find the world
in a moth's wing, you

might see a galaxy
in a sparkle of fireflies
lighting up the night

or glimpse the universe
in patterns of a snowflake,
fleeting, endlessly unique.

This is how the world works:
small and humble,
dazzling, sharp

lenses made to remedy
our tendency to
blindness

Death of an Oak

By Casey Mills

Oh to be gentle
   when they are unkind
   to remember our safety
   like the base of an oak

tree of centuries
   shedding acorns and leaves
   bread broken by all creatures
   feasting on the bounty

and when the chainsaw comes
   for no good reason whatsoever
   I will lift my limbs, expose my body
   and let the teeth bite

standing proud until I fall
   wearing forgiveness in the ridges
   of the gray bark we all ate from
   when the winter grew cold.

The Woman Who Loved a Tree

By Gabrielle Munslow

for Gabrielle — and the parts of her still blooming

She loved once.
Not fiercely.
Not loudly.
But completely.

It wasn't a man.
Not really.
It was a tree.

She found it—
small, broken-limbed, barely green.
And she—
full of marrow and music—
fed it with everything.

She brought water in her cupped hands.
Sang lullabies into its bark.
Told no one.
Not even herself.

And the tree grew.
And she... dimmed.

She didn't ask for shade.
Didn't beg for fruit.
She only wanted it to stand.

One day—
bone-thin, bird-quiet—
she took the ribbon from her throat
and tied herself gently
to the place where limb met wind.

It wasn't a cry for help.
It was a return.

And in that moment—
soft as dusk—
she did not fall.

She became bark.
She became root.
She became pulse beneath the soil.

And the tree—
still blooming—
remembers her.

They say it was death.
But it wasn't.

It was the moment
the tending ended.
And the becoming began.

They became one.
And love—
true love—
never needed a witness.

River Visions

By Tina Nakae

Mud curves along slag rock sharp, piercing.
Wild winds hug tight to canyon walls, kissing
green swallows that sift along grainy, ocher cliffs.

Ruined and bruised, clear eyes tremble.
Sighs echo deep through granite, waves
curl swarming toward brilliance.

Tamaracks clutter the bank ragged, worn to bright white.
A milky, wan sun ripples atop the water,
while soft, blue belief swings carelessly on a cloud.

What brings us here?
Where will we gather
when the time comes?

Beneath the Canopy

By Deborah Ramos

The Amazon scared me,
but not the greens of ferns and philodendrons,
not the pinks of the shy river dolphins,
not the orange fruit of the dripping sunset.
It was the not knowing.

How would I survive the orchestra
of bubbly fluids in my guts?
The constricted pounding behind my eyes?
Or the monkey mind of an insomniac?
I had the pharmacy of pills in my bag,
and still, I was feverish.

Beneath a canopy of macaw reds and toucan yellows,
anxiety settled in the seat of a canoe
motoring down the river road.
A butterfly with tissue-paper wings
brushed my face and rested
on the walnut brown skin of our guide.
I was becoming a part of the painting.

While we explored leaf-cutter trails,
cleaned yucca roots to make bread,
and sipped the shaman's brew of ayahuasca,
behemoth cockroaches filled
every cranny of our open bags and shoes.
The prehistoric scarabs
will miss my screams the most.

But it was the blue jungle rains
that slowed the pumping of my heart,
and the carbon sink of new air
that quieted the static in my head.
I surrendered to the peace of it,
to the simplicity of it,
I surrendered until the aging core of my body
fell into the chanting hands of the Amazon.

The Spider Walks a Tightrope

By Christie Chandler Stahl

An orb weaver on the edge of the world
launches a silken strand, an airy whirl
wind whipped, a thread of chance.
It catches a pine branch, a knot pulled taut,
an anchor tougher than an oak's root.
Threads of silk, a compass spun.
She measures each silent chord,
strengthening and stretching
her spiral sphere.
Gusts burst through,
the web gives, bends, sways,
dancing strength,
a forgiving sail against
an unforgiving wind.
The storm passes, the web shimmers
in dewy morning calm.
A tiny shadow neatly wrapped
waits nearby.

Gentle Disturbance

By Cathy Symes

Place your ear on the earth
and listen to its indifference.
The soil's silent threads of tender succour
woven out towards itself.
Looking upwards
towards leaf bare branches
set against cloud white sky
watching spaces
laced between needle thin ends.
Each carrying buds
hard scaled coverings of sap green leaves
folded in layers, waiting for light to emerge.

You understand I think, the purpose of leaves fallen
their flattened stems and red brown catkins
disparate and immotile, all of them rotting.
A bruised reclamation of fragmented shredding's
an understanding shared.

There is nothing that it asks of us but this.

Earth Amulet Poetry Prize

by

River Paw Press

Contributor Bios

Maryam Imogen Ghouth is a literary artist working across written, audio, and visual poetry. Her written work has appeared in several literary journals, including *inScribe, Science Write Now, Last Leaves, Querencia Press,* and others. Her poetry recordings have been used as overlays in award-winning short films, such as *Under the Sun* by director Alla Dulh. Her poetry films, such as *Not Alone,* have been screened and awarded at over 30 international film festivals. She has published a chapbook titled *I Ask My Being: Reflective Poems on Staying True,* which includes an album of her narrated poems set to neoclassical music.

Vinita Agrawal lives in Indore, India. She has authored six books of poetry and edited two anthologies on climate change. She is the recipient of the Jayanta Mahapatra National Award for Literature 2024, the Proverse Prize Hongkong 2021, and the Rabindranath Tagore Literary Prize 2018. She co-edits the Yearbook series of Indian Poetry in English. She has been published in *Global South, Pratik, Mascara Review, Indian Literature, Asian Cha, Voice and Verse, The Bombay Literary Magazine* and the *Knopf Newsletter* among others. She is on the Advisory Board of the Tagore Literary Prize.
www.vinitawords.com

Scott W. Westcott is a poet, journalist and writer living in Erie, Pennsylvania. He draws inspiration from time spent outdoors, with family, or anywhere his phone is not. He turns to poetry to try to seek calm and clarity amid the ever-growing chaos in which we exist.

Alexander "Al" Scott Pearce Baker is a naturalist based in Nova Scotia. His fiction has appeared in *Dark Harbor* and *Flash Phantoms,* his poetry in The *Lucky Lizard* and *Marrow Magazine,* and his academic work with publishers including Routledge, Palgrave Macmillan, and Bloomsbury.

Jharna Choudhury, author of the Assamese poetry collection Kaya (2023), is a hand embroidery artist from Assam, India, who goes by the name "Embroidery Stories." Her creative writings have found home in *Ethelzine, Parcham, Thumbprint Northeast, Pine Cone Review, SETU, The Little Journal of Northeast India, Muse India, WILDsound, Spillwords,* and in nine anthologies (Indie Blu(e) Publishing, Authorspress, and others). Her poetry explores the body, memory, ecology, intergenerational trauma, illness, cultural identity, weaving language into textile and felt experience. She is also an Assistant Professor of English Literature at Dimoria College, Khetri, Assam, India.

Diane Funston writes poetry of nature and human nature. She co-founded a women's poetry salon in San Diego, created a weekly poetry gathering in the high desert town of Tehachapi, CA and most recently has been the Yuba-Sutter Arts and Culture Poet-in-Residence for the past two years. It is in this role she created Poetry Square, a monthly online venue that features poets from all the world reading their work and discussing creative process. Her first chapbook, "Over the Falls", was published in 2022 by Foothills Publishing. Diane is also a visual artist in mosaic, wool felting, and collage.

Gloria Heffernan's most recent poetry collection is *Fused* (Shanti Arts Publishing). Her craft book, *Exploring Poetry of Presence* (Back Porch Productions) won the CNY Book Award for Nonfiction. She received the 2022 Naugatuck River Review Narrative Poetry Prize. Gloria is the author of the collections *Peregrinatio: Poems for Antarctica* (Kelsay Books), and *What the Gratitude List Said to the Bucket List*, (New York Quarterly Books). To learn more, visit: www.gloriaheffernan.wordpress.com.

Larry Kilman is an American poet and journalist from New York who has spent more time outside of the US than within, living in Paris, Hong Kong, Munich, Frankfurt and currently in Johannesburg, none of it planned. He is therefore a believer in the power of serendipity and being open to the unexpected. His poems have appeared in a wide variety of publications, including Superpresent, Mudfish, Epiphany, Brief Wilderness, and Thorn & Bloom. He is a faculty member of the American Graduate School in Paris.

Margie B. Klein has been a nature writer for 35 years. With a career in the fields of natural resources protection and environmental education, she has expressed her passion for the environment through poems, essays, articles and stories. Her work has been published in many venues including Impermanent Earth, Plants and Poetry Journal, and others. She is a fellow with the International League of Conservation Writers and has won the Conservation Education Writing Award from The Wildlife Society. She is a member of the Nevada Poetry Society.

Molly O'Dell is a family physician and loves being outdoors, her primary influencer. She also loves writing and received an MFA from University of Nebraska in 2009 and published a chapbook, *Off the Chart* and a multi-genre collection, *Care is A Four Letter Verb* thanks to the regional and national literary journal editors who published her poems. *Unsolicited 96 Saws and Quips* in the Wake of the Pandemic was published for her public health colleagues in 2021. She currently serves as poetry editor for the *Journal of Medical Humanities*.

Caroline Anne Pollard is a poet based in Lancashire, whose work navigates the intersections of spiritual transformation and ecological disintegration. Her poetry combines lyrical intensity with visions of spiritual transformation through the degradation of nature. Pollard questions the ethics of conceiving aesthetics in a post-apocalyptic landscape. Rather than aestheticising degradation for its own sake, she questions our ethical and emotional relationship with polluted landscapes. Her poetry asks: What does it mean to love a landscape that has been changed through human intervention? And more urgently: Does what remains become more sacred?

Stephen Sanders is a poet who writes in many voices. First published in 1975, Sanders has become an award-winning poet with book, magazine, and anthology credits too numerous to list here. He is the current president of the Fort Worth Poetry Society and is an active member of the Poetry Society of Texas. You can find examples of his work on YouTube at "The Adventure Poetry Channel." If you want to know more about him, simply do a web search for "Stephen Sanders poetry."

Ron Shapiro is a recipient of Cornell University's Outstanding Teacher Award. He has published writings in *The Whole Word Catalogue, More Strategies for Teaching Writing, NoVa Bards 2022 through 2025, Gatherings, Poets of the Promise, Minute Musings, Poetry X Hunger, All Your Poems, Spilled Ink, Walt Whitman 205 Anthology, Backchannels, Paper Cranes Literary Magazine, TheNewVerse.News, Gezer Gallery, Zest of the Lemon*, two chapbooks: *Sacred Spaces, Wonderings and Understory*, a nature poetry book. He lives with his wife Rikki and Shanti, their cat, in Reston, Virginia.

Jonathan Chibuike Ukah is a Pushcart Prize-nominated poet from the UK with his family. His poems have been featured in the *Atticus Review, San Antonio Review, The Ephemeral Literary Review, Strange Horizons, The Pierian, The Unleash Lit* and elsewhere. He is the winner of the Alexander Pope Poetry Award 2023 and the second runner-up of the Wingless Dreamer Publishing Poetry Prize 2023.

William Weissinger's poem *Bear With Salmon* was recently published in The Madrona Project's Empty Bowl Cookbook, which includes work from many of the Northwest's best poets. His poem *The Best Apple Crisp You'll Ever Have* will be published in the Fall Menu of Malarkey Books. In addition to poetry, he writes fiction. His flash fiction has won several prizes. He is a retired attorney who lives on San Juan Island in Washington State, where he also sculpts stone. His work focuses on animals of the Pacific Northwest, especially salmon. See his sculptures at: WeissingerStudios.com

Diane Bier is a binge reader who always has a book or camera in hand. Her writing reflects her passion for social change and social issues. She has an MFA from William Paterson University, participates in several writing communities where she writes and studies. Her work has been published in various literary journals. Diane Bier resides in NJ with her family and dog where she enjoys gardening and walking.

Charles C. Gaines is a recently retired general dentist, former gunfighter, teacher and coach, who is finally free to spend time crafting poetry. He is a member of the Fort Worth Poetry Society. He finds his inspiration in everything from thoughts and emotions to observations in walking the city, visiting new places and spending time alone in nature. At 74, he believes he is just now beginning to fulfill his dreams.

Rebecca Herz is a poet, wife, mom, cat lover, and school-based therapist. Her 2023 book, Homecoming and other poems, along with her social media content, can be found on linktr.ee/rebeccaherz. Her latest poetry collection, *Locus of Control*, 2026, can be found on the Prolific Pulse Website with links for purchase. https://www.prolificpulse.com/rebeccaherz.3

Doc Janning is the 82 year-old Inaugural Poet Laureate of The City of South Euclid, Ohio, Third Poet Laureate of Cuyahoga County, Ohio, and Poet Laureate of the congregation to which he belongs. He has had poems included in 36 anthologies and many other publications. His first book of poetry, "Before Today ∞ Beyond Tomorrow, Poems from the Multiverse", was published by Venetian Spider Press, on November 27, 2023 and includes two poems nominated for a Pushcart Prize.

Maryna Krazhova is a Belarusian-born American poet based in the Boston area, Massachusetts. Her works often explore themes of memory, language, and identity, as well as the natural world, blending lyricism with subtle irony. She has been published in *New Feathers* Anthology, *Other Side of Hope*, *Haiku Shack Magazine*, *Blood and Bourbon*, and several Belarusian and Polish magazines.

Elizabeth Iannaci is a widely published poet who grew up in the Los Angeles area in a time when acres of orange groves & strawberry fields lined the 10 freeway. She earned her Poetry MFA from Vermont College of Fine Arts, and is partially sighted, which may account for her preference for paisley over polka dots. Her work appeared recently in *Women in a Golden State*, *Midwestern Miscellany*, *Interlitq*, *Discretionary Love*, among others. Her latest chapbook is *The Virgin Turtle Light Show: Spring, 1968* (Latitude 34 Press).

Mariana Mcdonald is a poet, writer, and activist. Her poetry, fiction, essays, and journalism have appeared in many journals and anthologies, including, *Cutthroat, Sargasso, Crab Orchard Review, The New Verse News, Antología de la Poesía Viequense, Anthology of Southern Poets, About Place Journal,* and *The Longridge Review.* She was named a Hambidge Arts Center fellow in 2012 and appointed a Black Earth Institute Scholar/Fellow in 2022. She lives in Atlanta.

Casey Mills writes poems early in the morning while his kids sleep. He lives in Northern California next to a creek he enjoys spending time with. His poetry has been published in *California Quarterly, Tule Review, Amethyst Review, Calla Press*, and elsewhere. You can read more of his poems at: caseymillspoems.com.

Gabrielle Marie Munslow is a UK-based poet and nurse practitioner whose work explores survival, ecological grief, and the intersections between human life and the natural world. Her poetry has appeared in *Neon Origami, Bristol Noir,* and *The Ekphrastic Review.* She is currently developing several themed collections, including *What I Made from the Ruins and Phoenix-Souled,* while actively submitting work to international journals and prizes. Drawing on both her clinical practice and lived experience, Gabrielle writes with a focus on resilience, myth, and the enduring bond between humanity and the natural world.

Tina Nakae is a poet and teacher based in Trout Lake, Washington. Her poems have appeared in local newspapers, *Mad Persona Literary Magazine, Masque and Spectacle* and *Trashlight Press.* This Spring her poetry will appear in two anthologies; *Sublimation* and *Earth Amulet.* She loves to read aloud at local events to celebrate the power of words with community.

Deborah Ramos, a San Diego artist and poet, is the author of from the earthen drum of my body. She writes about the sacred feminine, primal desires, roadkill, and her cats. Deborah's poetry has appeared in publications such as, *SageWoman, Rattlesnake Press, National Beat* Anthology, Border Voices, San Diego's Writers Ink, South Broadway Ghost Society, and more. She is a co-founder and art curator of the *Electric Womb*, dedicated to promote and support womyn artists. Her creative life includes traveling, writing, exhibiting her art and photography, and hosting Poets at the Grove readings in Balboa Park, San Diego.

Christie Chandler Stahl is a former librarian who writes poetry, stories and facilitates writing workshops. Her poems have appeared or are forthcoming in *Midwest Review, The Ekphrastic Review, Flying Island Journal, The Winged*

Moon Literary Journal, and others. She lives in Evanston, Illinois, is a Butterfly Monitor, and loves gardening, hiking, photography and swimming in Lake Michigan.

Cathy Symes is a poet and writer living in Nottingham, England. Her poetry has been published by the *Dawntreader* magazine and online by *Ink Sweat and Tears* and *Green Ink Poetry*. Her short fiction was long listed for the 2024 Aurora Prize.

~~~~~
~~~~~

Kalpna Singh-Chitnis is an Indian-American poet, writer, filmmaker, and author of seven poetry collections, including *Love Letters to Ukraine from Uyava* (River Paw Press, 2023), recipient of the prestigious Hryhorii Kochur Award—a State Award of Ukraine—for its bilingual edition translated by Volodymyr Tymchuk, a poet and Lt. Colonel in the Armed Forces of Ukraine, and a finalist for the 2023 International Book Awards. Her other notable works include *Trespassing My Ancestral Lands* (Finishing Line Press, 2024), shortlisted for the 2024-2025 Rabindranath Tagore Literary Prize and *Bare Soul*, which earned her the 2017 Naji Naaman Literary Prize, along with four poetry collections in Hindi. She curated and edited *Sunflowers: Ukrainian Poetry on War, Resistance, Hope, and Peace*, shortlisted for the 2023 National Indie Excellence Award. A Pushcart Prize nominee, her poems have been translated into twenty-one languages. Her awards and honors include the Paestum International Poetry Prize, Rajiv Gandhi Global Excellence Award, Bihar Shri, and the Bihar Rajbhasha Parishad Award, given by the Government of Bihar, India. Her poems and poetry film *River of Songs*, archived in the Lunar Codex, were sent to the Moon's south pole with NASA–SpaceX–Intuitive Machines–Firefly Aerospace missions in 2024–2025.

A former lecturer of International Relations, Kalpna Singh-Chitnis studied Political Science at Magadh University, Bodhgaya, India, and Buddhism Through Its Scriptures at HarvardX (Harvard University). She is also an alumna of the Silk Routes Project, International Writing Program, University of Iowa (2014–2016), and her work has appeared or been reviewed and featured in *World Literature Today, Columbia Journal, The Los Angeles Review, Poetry International, Tupelo Quarterly, Cold Mountain Review, Indian Literature, Vsesvit, Life in Quarantine* (Stanford University), and others. Her poetry has earned praise from Dr. Wazir Agha, a nominee for the Nobel Prize in Literature; Amrita Pritam, recipient of the Vaptsarov Award and Ordre des Arts et des Lettres; and Gulzar, a poet, Academy Award-winning lyricist, and filmmaker. She has been referenced in *The New York Times* and *Huffington Post*, and featured in *The Telegraph, The Examiner, OC Register, Los Angeles Times, Daily Pilot*, and others.

Kalpna Singh-Chitnis works as an independent filmmaker in Hollywood and is known for her feature film *Goodbye My Friend* and short films *Girl with an Accent* and *The Tree*, among others. She is also the Editor-in-Chief of *Life and Legends*, publisher and editor at River Paw Press, and serves as an Advocacy Member of the United Nations Association of the USA. Website: <u>www.kalpnasinghchitnis.com</u>.

More from River Paw Press

One Thousand Origami Paper Cranes Fly Away

(Winner of the 2025 Silent River Poetry Prize)
by Martin Willitts Jr.

Hutsulka

(2025 Silent River Poetry Prize Finalist)
by Nicole Yurcaba

Dead Boys I Have Known

(2025 Silent River Poetry Prize Semi-Finalist)
by Joanna Grant

Sunflowers: Ukrainian Poetry on War Resistance, Hope and Peace

(2023 National Indie Excellence Award)
edited by
Kalpna Singh-Chitnis

Love Letters to Ukraine from Uyava

(Winner of the 2024 Hryhorii Kochur Award, conferred by the State of Ukraine)
by Kalpna Singh-Chitnis

Also available in a bilingual English–Ukrainian edition

Любовні листи до України від Уяви

Калпна Сінг-Чітніс

Переклав

Володимир Тимчук